A TOURIST GUIDE TO KOS' TOWNS AND
THE COUNTRYSIDE - MUSEUMS
ARCHELOGICAL SITES
WITH MAPS - EXCURSIONS - WALKS

KOS

EDITIONS : MARMATAKIS BROTHERS
PAZINOS AKROTIRI - CHANIA 73100 CRETE
TEL - FAX : 28210 - 66290

CONTENTS

CONTENTS

Routes in Kos Island

I swear by Apollo the physician, and Aesculapius, and Health, and All-heal, and all the gods and goddesses, that, according to my ability and judgment, I will keep this Oath and this stipulation

To reckon him who taught me this Art equally dear to me as my parents, to share my substance with him, and relieve his necessities if required; to look upon his offspring in the same footing as my own brothers, and to teach them this art, if they shall wish to learn it, without fee or stipulation;

And that by precept, lecture, and every other mode of instruction, I will impart knowledge of the Art to my own sons, and those of my teachers, and to disciples bound by a stipulation and oath according to the law of medicine, but to none others.

I will follow that system of regimen, which according to my ability and judgment, I consider for the benefit of my patients, and abstain from whatever is deleterious and mischievous........

From **Hippocrates' Oath**

The founder of Medicine was born 2,500 years ago in Kos island. His ethics was of such an extent, that he established the ethic code of medical profession, which is used till nowadays when students graduate medicine.

Geographical Position And Morphology

Among the precious stones which adorn the Aegean Sea, **Dodecanese Islands** have a special place since, except for their beauty, they have been the meeting point between East and West, integrated different cultures and created their own ones.

Kos is the third largest island of the Dodecanese after Rhodes and Karpathos. It lies between Nissyros and Kalymnos at the opening of *Kerameikos bay* which is formed by *Alikarnassos* and *Knidos* peninsulas

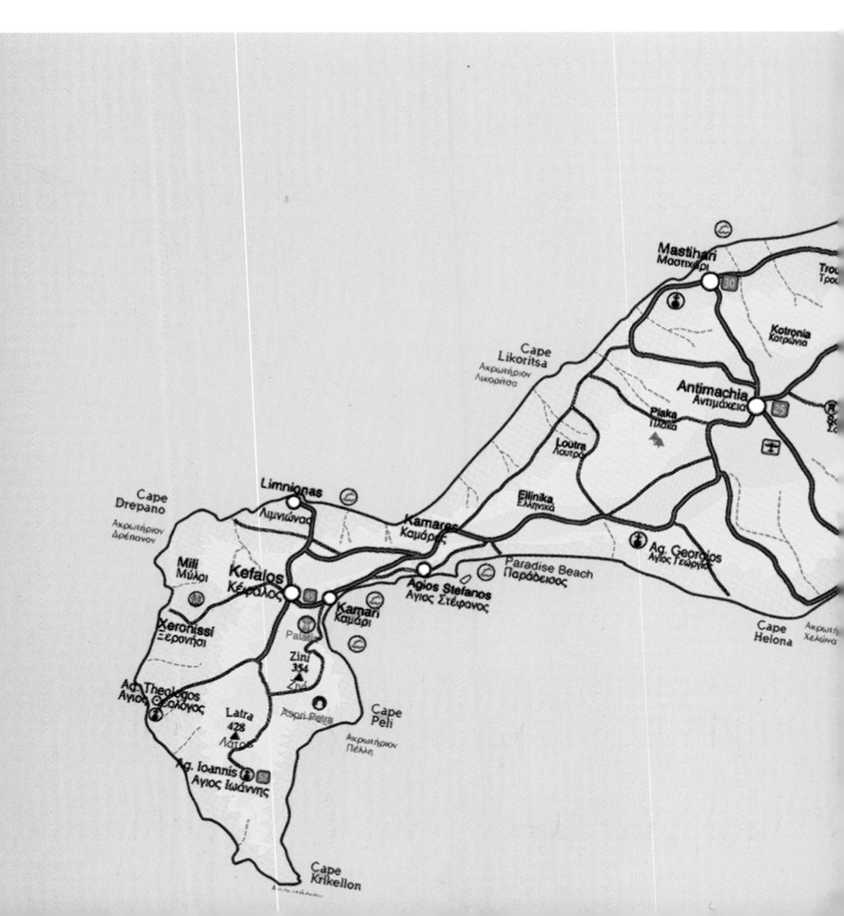

and is located 4 n. miles off the opposite coast of Asia Minor.

The island's area is 290 sq. km. Kos has an oblong shape of 45 km long and is between 2 and 11 km large. Its coastline is 113 km long where many sandy beaches and bights are located, formed by the capes of *Skandari*, *Psalidi*, *Aghios Fokas*, *Krikelo*, *Drepano* and *Chelona*. The largest part of the island is flat while mountains such as **Dikaios** - called Oromedon in ancient Greek - (864m) and **Sympeiros** the lowest one (428m), are only situated at the eastern part of Kos. **Latra** hill (416m) is situated southwest.

Mild climate along with many streams

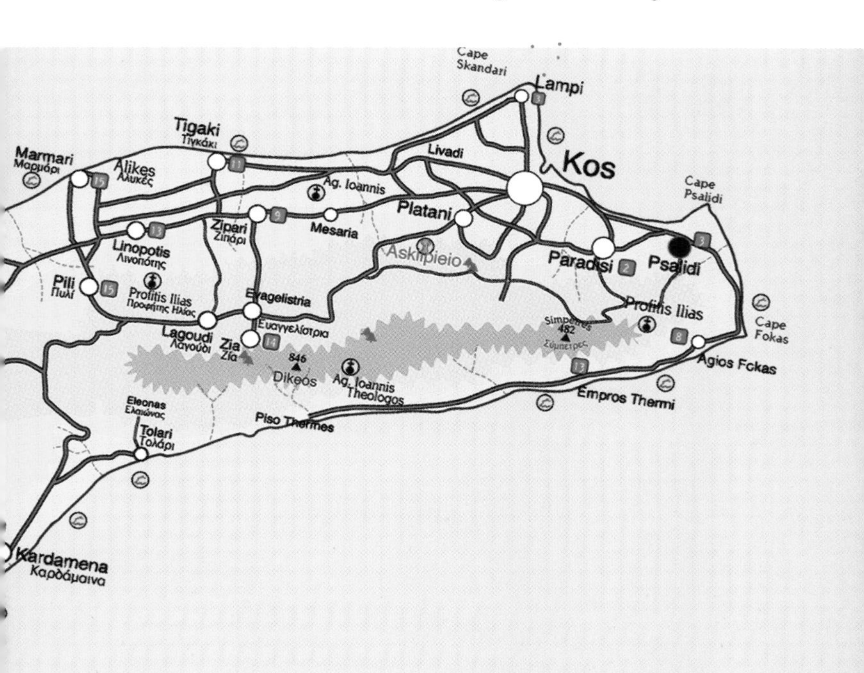

have created a fertile ground where excellent **vegetables** and **fruits** are cultivated while the island's vineyards produce an excellent semi-sweet **white wine**. There are five big and several smallest sponge-fishing firms, a dockyard for small ships as well as the only **salt pan** in Dodecanese where large quantities of salt are produced. The underground is rich in iron metals such as manganese, chromite, barite, perlite, etc. Kos has also

The beautiful Paradisos beach lying just before Kefalos bay, is well-known for its crystal-clear waters.

excellent spas which are very well organized.

The 27,000 inhabitants mostly work in merchant marine, fishery, cattle-breeding, farming, bee-farming and in small industries; yet, the skyrocketing development in tourism (Kos is the second financial and tourist center in Dodecanese after Rhodes) has changed the inhabitants' occupations and habits as well as the island's features.

Sea together with fishery and tourism represent important sources of wealth for the island.

MYTHOLOGY - NAME

The island's name and birth have been associated with very ancient and fascinating legends. According to one of them, *Gigantomachy* (the battle between gods and giants) finished with Giants' defeat. Yet, *Giant Polyvotis*, kept resisting and took refuge in Kos. God Poseidon persecuted him and cut a part of the island with his trident and crushed the giant, while *Nissyros*, the nearby island, was formed by the cut part. The first names of the island, i.e. **«Kynnis»** after the giant Konnis and **«Koia»** after the giant Koio, are associated with this legend. According to another tradition, the island has been named after the daughter of king *Meropas* the 2nd (or *Triopas* the 2nd), Koos (or Kos). Still, some researchers have claimed that the princess was named *Astypalaia*, which justifies one of the oldest names of the first capital on the island.

A third legend, extremely complicated, is associated with the colonization of the island by *Heraclides*. According to this legend, **Hercules** and his companions were shipwrecked in Kos where they succeeded in being rescued. Nevertheless, *Hercules* did not find a hospitable place there. Following an epic duel with the shepherd **Antagoras**, he took refuge in the mountainous area of the island (near today's *Pyli*) a place which was named *Fyxa* after Hercules' refuge (fygi). There, he found hospitable people and denounced the violation of **«Patrioi Xenoi»** (the holiness of hospitality). The inhabitants justified him and followed him to a victorious battle during which *Chalkiope*, the daughter of *Eurypilos*, was taken hostage. *Chalkiope's* union with *Hercules* gave birth to a son, *Thessalus Heraclides,* and two daughters, *Kalymnos* and

A relief representing Hercules shooting at the "Birds Stymphalides ". A work of the Hellenistic period, which is now being exposed at the Archeological Museum of Kos.

Leros. *Thessalus*' sons, *Phidippos* and *Antiphos*, led thirty ships wich took part in the Trojan War. Heraclides' association with Thessalus demonstrates the strong bonds, which have been relating people in Kos with those in Thessaly. It also proves the historical event, that of Kos being later colonized by Dorians of *Epidauros* (of Argolida), who have come from Thessaly and taken refuge in Argosand, and not by Dorians of Laconia.

Other names which have been associated with the island are **«Meropis»** after the legendery king *Meropas*, **«Karis»** probably

after Kares inhabitants but mostly after the ancient word «Karis» meaning shrimp because of the island's shape, **«Nymphaea»** after the numerous temples dedicated to the Nymphs, «Island of the blissful» due to the happiness and prosperity of the islanders, «Lango» a name given by the Knights of Saint John because of its shape, «Stankoe» a name given to the island during the Turkish occupation (a deformation of the phrase «is tin Ko»=to Kos). Yet, all these names have been forgotten and the more ancient one, Kos, has prevailed.

Foreground: Ruins of Pandimos Aphrodite's temple and at the background the mosque of Loggia (excavations in the port's area)

HISTORY

PREHISTORICAL PERIOD

The Neolithic settlement of Kos has proven that the island was inhabited as early as the 4th millennium BC. The first inhabitants were **Prohellens**, *Pelasgians,* and *Leleges* (as proven by the place-names *Astypalaia, Alasarna, Sitea*, but also by Pelasgian ruins of walls in *Aghios Fokas* and *Palaioskala*). Other people who have settled in Kos were Kares, Phoenicians. The latter's settlement has been proven by Phoenician tombs which have been found at the eastern part of the island. Also, around 1600 BC a group of **Minoan Cretans** came in the island and settled near the port (Serayia area). Relationships between Koans and Cretans were friendly and trade was boosted.

Later on, following the devastation of the Minoan civilization by the tidal wave which had been caused by the volcano's eruption in *Thira*, **Mycenaean people** arrived in the island and took over Cretans' colonies. Thus, Kos was influenced by their culture as proven by Mycenaean ruins found on the island. In *Homer's Iliad* we are being informed on Kos and the nearby islands' participation in the Trojan War with 30 ships under the leadership of *Phidippos* and *Antiphos* (the sons of Thessalus Heraclide). On their return home, ships were shipwrecked. Yet, *Podaleirios,* Asclepius' son, and his companions managed to arrive safe in the island where they established the worship of Asclepius the Therapist (Ietiros).

In the 11th century BC, when **Dorians** (of Epidaurus) expanded towards Southern Greece, they colonized Kos and the island experienced a new prosperous period in farming, trade, sailing and handicrafts.

Goddess Artemis bringing a quiver and an arch A hunting dog is sitting by her feet. A statue of the 2nd century BC, which was found in the residence where the mosaic "Kidnapping of Europe" was found.

According to *Strabon,* Dorians together with people of Rhodes established colonies in Southern Italy (Helpies). Doric writing and dialect as well as Doric worship habits and rituals prevailed in Kos. The worship of «Ietiros Asclepius» (Asclepius the Therapist), *Hercules, Demeter, Aphrodite,* and *Apollo* became extremely important. Most researchers have agreed on the fact that worship of Aclepius came in Kos directly from the Thessalic region of Trikki (today's Trikala), a very long time ago, perhaps in the 9th or 8th century BC.

HISTORICAL PERIOD

The island's most ancient capital has been named **Astypalaia** and its position has been identified with the seaside place called «Palatia», near the village *Kefalos.* The political regime was first monarchy and later on, oligarchy. During the 7th and 6th

Kefalos bay area where the most ancient capital on the island has been located.

centuries BC political institutions were modified in all Greek area. In Kos, power shifted from the «Archons» (Nobles) to the **«Ecclesea tou Dimou»** (Assembly of the people). Democracy was established and a congress, a parliament and all the spectrum of the democratic institutions were created.

In the 7th century BC, a very important event took place in the island which had already started thriving. **«Doric Exapolis»**, a federation of six cities, *Kos, Knidos Alicarnassos* and three cities of Rhodes - *Lindos, Ialyssos and Kameiros* - was created which had a military, political, economic and religious character. Its center was the temple of *Triopios Apollo* located at the opposite cape of Asia Minor, where religious ceremonies were jointly celebrated and races used to take place, such as the «Doric race» to honor Apollo. Kos prospered and

The two restored columns of the ancient forum in Kos town.

developed in every field.

At the end of the 6th century BC, the Persians who had already expanded till the coasts of Asia Minor, did not spare Kos' that was transformed into a Persian Satrapy. In the beginning, relationships with the conquerors were relatively good. Yet, when Persians demanded Kos participation for attacking continental Greece, Koans refused. Then, the cruel reign of *queen Artemisia*, the Satrap of Alicarnassos, was imposed. Artemisia forced the Koans to built five ships which were added to the Persian fleet. Yet, following Persians' defeat in Salamis, Plataea and the naval battle in Mycale, Kos together with the rest of the Ionic coasts and the nearby islands got rid of the Persian rulers (475 BC). During that period, around 500 BC, Kos stroke its first silver coin which beared a sea cancer (crab) on one side, the symbol of the island, and Asclepius or Apollo or even Hercules and the word «Koion» on the other side. After 480 BC, Attic tetradrachms and later on, those of Rhodes were put in circulation.

After Koan people persecuted Persians off the island, Kos became member of the 1st Athenian Alliance. When the **Peloponnesian War** started (431 - 404 BC), Koans, although Dorians, sided with Athenians, since they were members of the Alliance. In 411 BC, the Spartan army arrived in the island's capital and conquered and looted the city. Many inhabitants left the island and settled in a nearby small island that they named Astypalaia. A terrible earthquake completed Kos' devastation. Athenians sent financial help and General Alcibiades who fortified the city. A civil dispute between democrat and oligarchic partisans occurred in the island which had to side with one of these

A bust of a man who is holding dogs on his chest. A work dating back to the Roman period (Archeologica l Museum of Kos).

groups. By the end of the Peloponnesian War and the victory of Spartans, the democratic regime was abolished and «Decarchy» was imposed. When all these adventures finished, the island managed to rise again. Mostly after the establishment of the new capital of Kos (365 - 364 BC), it managed to thrive again both in sailing and trade. It

The wonderful mosaic, which represents Asclepius' arrival in the island of Kos where he is being welcomed by an inhabitant and Hippocrates who is sitting on a rock.

became member of the Athenian Alliance. Kos later sided with Philip and then with Alexander, following Macedonians' rising in power.

During the **Hellenistic period**, that of Alexander's successors, the city and all the area continued prospering. There were more than 160,000 inhabitants in Kos while trade, sailing, pottery, arts and humanities were at their peak while the heavy Doric dialect moved back and left its place to the refined Alexandrian. Kos became part of the *state of Antigonos* although from times to times, Koans sided with Ptolemeus' dynasty, depending on who was the most powerful. When the Roman power appeared, Koans accompanied by Rhodes and the king of Pergamus, Attalus, sided with them, against *Philip the 5th*, King of Macedonia, and they won at the famous battle of Kynos Kefales.

In 88 BC, the king of Pontus, **Mithridates** seized the island and treated it with an extreme cruelty. In 82 BC, Romans chassed Mithridates and made Kos and surrounding islands, a **Roman province**. Yet, T*iberius* granted special privileges to the island, such as asylum and tax exemption as far as Asclepium was concerned. Despite that, the island experienced an unprecedented looting as it was deprived from its artistic treasures, which were to decorate Rome. The island was further devastated by a terrible earthquake which took place probably in the 6th or 5th century BC.

Later on, Christianity begun spreading on the island and despite persecutions by Romans it rapidly expanded. *Saint Paul* too, passed from Kos.

BYZANTINE PERIOD

During the Byzantine period, Kos belonged to the **«Thema of Dodecanese»** and thus followed the tremendous fate of the Byzantine Empire. In 467 BC, *Vandals* looted and destroyed the island. In 500 BC, *Visigoths* lead by *Alaric*, further ruined the island. Raids kept on, mostly by Slavs (527

The statue of goddess Tyche, a work made in the Hellenistic period. (Archeological Museum of Kos).

AD) and Arabs, which brought new sufferings. In 554 AD, a terrible earthquake completely devastated the town, Asclepium and villages, while ground subsided by around one meter. The island kept on being attacked by *Saracen pirates* (612 AD), Norman ones, and others while in 1160 AD, it was temporarily conquered by Crusaders.

In 1204 AD, following *Constantinople's* seize by the Latin, the island passed under the **rule of Venetians**. Kos and the rest of the islands became part of the Ducat of the Aegean Sea and the Venetian *Leon Gavalas* proclaimed himself Duke. In 1262 AD, the Byzantine Emperor, *Michael Palaiologos* reconquered the island and annexed it to the Byzantine territories. Nevertheless, the Byzantine Empire was declining and Palaiologos was forced to cede the island to the Genovese as they had earlier offered him some help. During 1312 AD, Catalan - Spaniard Arabs repeatedly looted the island.

A blazon of the Knights period, built in a medieval castle in Kos.

THE ERA OF SAINT JOHN'S KNIGHTS

In 1304 AD, the Genovese archon of the region sold Kos, Rhodes and other territories to the order of **Saint John's Knights of Jerusalem** who arrived in the island in 1315 AD accompanied by their Grand Master, *Foulques de Villaret*. The sovereignty of the Knights lasted 218 years. The Knights fortified the island by constructing big fortification works, organized the army and the fleet and governed according to the order's rules. Their representatives exercised administration, as their headquarters was located in Rhodes. On the other hand, Koans who never sided with them were compelled, among others things, to provide them annually, with a warship.

In 1457 and in 1464 AD, *Turks* who had already destroyed the Byzantine Empire tried to seize the island. The inhabitants together with the Knights strongly resisted and managed to repulse them.

THE TURKISH OCCUPATION

In 1523 AD, *Sultan Suleyman the Magnificent*, who had already taken over Rhodes, managed to conquer the island despite heroic resistance displayed by Koans. Following an agreement, the Knights left the island with all their belongings, while Greeks suffered all the rage of Turks. During that dark period which lasted for 390 years, the inhabitants experienced massacres, humiliations, were diminished in number due to children kidnappings and many of them died of a torturing death for not changing their religion. Nevertheless, they managed to keep their faith intact

and to take part in the liberating combats of the Greek nation. Many Koans jointed the *Filiki Etaireia* (Revolutionary Organization) and strongly participated in the Greek Revolution in 1821. As a retaliation, the Turks hang 92 notables from Hippocrates' plane tree and many others all over the island.

The Administration Center (Dioikitirion), a building typical of the Italian ruling period.

THE ITALIAN RULE

On May 7, 1912, Kos together with all Dodecanese Islands, were placed under the Italian rule. Italians debarked on the island and stated that they had come to liberate the island from the Turks. The inhabitants welcomed them with enthusiasm. At first, cohabitation was friendly. Yet, the rise in fascism in Italy changed their politics and governors started oppressing the locals. In 1938, the Italian governor of Rhodes, *G M De Vecchi* transferred thirty magnificent mosaics from Kos to Rhodes, most of them from the Odeon as well as many other statues, when he was renovating the palace of the Grand Masters.

This cultural destruction coupled with Italians' will to give an intense Roman, Medieval and grotesque character to all buildings they were building, completely changed the island's face. Still, it is worth mentioning that great Italian architects made remarkable and extremely charming buildings, preserved and renovated many archeological sites and gave to the town of Kos (and to that of Rhodes) this aura of wealth which has made it, along with Rhodes, so special.

In 1943, following the fall of Italy during the World War II, *Germans* seized the island. Koans suffered all the hardships, well - known in Europe. In 1945, after the end of the war, the *British* conquered Kos and established a military administration.

UNIFICATION WITH GREECE

On March 7, 1948, according to the Treaty of Paris, unification of Dodecanese Islands with Greece was signed and the much - expected moment when a Greek flag would be raised on the island finally came.

HUMANITIES - SCIENCES

In Kos intellectual creators are numerous and particularly important as far as their offer to humanities is concerned. They excelled during the late classical period and mostly during Hellenistic years, i.e. during Alexander's successors' era.

Among them, we can distinguish ***Epimarchus***, author of comedies and founder of the Sicilian comedy, ***Ermesinactus***, poet of elegies, ***Herondas***, a poet, ***Philitas***, a scholar and teacher of Ptolemeus, ***Ariston***, philosopher of the Peripatetic School and ***Xenocritus*** who had successfully commented on Hippocrates' treatises.

Yet, the major and most important

Odeum. An edifice built in the 2nd century AD following the shape of ancient theaters.

offer of Kos to humanity was development in medicine. In Kos, Medical science found its award and its glorification. The first medical school has been created there. Apart from Hippocrates whom a special mention is going to be made to, a great number of physicians, called ***Asclepiadae*** (Asclepius'

descendants), had practice medicine before and after him. The most famous ones, before Hippocrates' inno-vation, were ***Nevros Appolonides***, who had been the doctor of the Persian king *Artaxerxes* the 1st, ***Gnossidicus***, Hippo-crates' father and teacher, and ***Herodicus***, Hippocrates' teacher.

The temple of Apollo at Asclepium. A building of Corithian order, 2nd century BC.

HIPPOCRATES

This great physician and philosopher, founder of the medical science, was born in Kos on Agrianius 27 (November or January) in the year 460 BC. His father was **Gnossidicus** the Asclepiad doctor, who gave Hippocrates his first knowledge in medicine. His mother was **Phainarete**, descendant of Hercules. Hippocrates died in 375 or in 377 BC, at a very old age (104 or 108 years old) in *Larissa, Thessaly*. He first studied in the Asclepium of Kos and afterwards in that of Knidos (Ionia). His contact with various philosophers such as **Anaxagoras** of Miletos gave him the chance to study the «matter». In Asclepium of Ephesus he worked on natural phenomena and in Samos Island he learnt *Pythagoras'* theories thanks to the philosopher *Melissos.* **Democritus** taught him philosophy and the sophists *Gorgias* and *Leontios* taught him rhetoric art. On a continuous quest and enhancing of knowledge, he traveled to Egypt and Asia, and practiced medicine at the same time.

In 430 BC, during the first year of the Peloponnesian War a plague occurred in Athens and on Pericles' invitation, Hippocrates arrived in the city and saved Athenians from the devastating disease. The City of Athens honored Hippocrates by naming him equal Athenian citizen; he had the right to eat in Pretaneum, he was initiated into the Eleusian mysteries (the second one after Hercules), he was offered a golden wreath and privileges were granted to young Koans as well as equal citizenship to his fellow - citizens.

The most important innovation made by Hippocrates was that he first

Statue of the Hellenistic period, probably representing Hippocrates. It has been found during the excavations in Odeum, (Archelogical Museum of Kos).

dispensed medicine from oracles and sorcerers. In other words, he made a distinction between medicine and religion and set the bases for a rational scientific research. He was the first who **classified** diseases and showed **methods of diagnosis** and **treatment** (according to *Galen*, he was the introducer of methodical treatment). Despite all sub-standard knowledge of that period he made excellent discoveries as far as the nature and treatment of diseases are concerned which even today astonish us on how large, accurate and applicable can be (for instance, almost 300 substances are mentioned in his pharmacology which constitute the basis for many drugs today). His knowledge on how to avoid infections, on hemostasis as well as surgery, especially in the field of obstetrics and gynecology, are even today considered unrivalled. His value has been recognized and is uncontested indeed, although many people have been appropriating his discoveries through centuries (mostly scientists in the 19th and 20th centuries).

Among the treatises he had written only 57 have survived which can be classified as follows: a) General (Oath, Aphorisms, Law, On Ancient Medicine), b) On the Articulation, c) On Regimen in Acute Diseases d) Pathology,e) The Book of Prognostics, f) On Special Nosology g) On Healing, h) On the Surgery i) On Ophthalmology j) On Gynacology k) On Obstetrics, l) On the Nature of the Child, m) Various. Hippocrates's rules are mostly mentioned in **«Aphorismi»** a basic medical treatise even up till the 18th century.

Hippocrates' unrest nature was not only

HIPPOCRATES OATH

I. I SWEAR BY APOLLO THE PHYSICIAN, AND AESCULAPIUS, AND HEALTH, AND ALL-HEAL, AND ALL THE GODS AND GODDESSES, THAT, ACCORDING TO MY ABILITY AND JUDGMENT, I WILL KEEP THIS OATH AND THIS STIPULATION

II. TO RECKON HIM WHO TAUGHT ME THIS ART EQUALLY DEAR TO ME AS MY PARENTS, TO SHARE MY SUBSTANCE WITH HIM, AND RELIEVE HIS NECESSITIES IF REQUIRED TO LOOK UPON HIS OFFSPRING IN THE SAME FOOTING AS MY OWN BROTHERS, AND TO TEACH THEM THIS ART, IF THEY SHALL WISH TO LEARN IT, WITHOUT FEE OR STIPULATION

III. AND THAT BY PRECEPT, LECTURE, AND EVERY OTHER MODE OF INSTRUCTION, I WILL IMPART KNOWLEDGE OF THE ART TO MY OWN SONS, AND THOSE OF MY TEACHERS, AND TO DISCIPLES BOUND BY A STIPULATION AND OATH ACCORDING TO THE LAW OF MEDICINE, BUT TO NONE OTHERS.

IV. I WILL FOLLOW THAT SYSTEM OF REGIMEN, WHICH ACCORDING TO MY ABILITY AND JUDGMENT, I CONSIDER FOR THE BENEFIT OF MY PATIENTS, AND ABSTAIN FROM WHATEVER IS DELETERIOUS AND MISCHIEVOUS.

V. I WILL GIVE NO DEADLY MEDICINE TO ANY ONE IF ASKED, NOR SUGGEST ANY SUCH COUNSEL AND IN LIKE MANNER I WILL GIVE TO A WOMAN A PESSARY TO PRODUCE ABORTION.

VI. WITH PURITY AND WITH HOLINESS I WILL PASS MY LIFE AND PRACTICE MY ART.

VII. I WILL NOT CUT PERSONS LABORING UNDER THE STONE, BUT WILL LEAVE THIS TO BE DONE BY MEN WHO ARE PRACTITIONERS OF THIS WORK.

IIX. INTO WHATEVER HOUSES I ENTER, I WILL GO INTO THEM FOR THE BENEFIT OF THE SICK, AND WILL ABSTAIN FROM EVERY VOLUNTARY ACT OF MISCHIEF AND CORRUPTION AND, FURTHER FROM THE SEDUCTION OF FEMALES AND SLAVES.

IX. WHATEVER, IN CONNECTION WITH IT, I SEE OR HEAR, IN THE LIFE OF MEN, WHICH OUGHT NOT TO BE SPOKEN OF ABROAD, I WILL NOT DIVULGE, AS RECKONING THAT SUCH SHOULD BE KEPT SECRET.

X. WHILE I CONTINUE TO KEEP THIS OATH INVIOLATE, MAY IT BE GRANTED TO ME TO ENJOY LIFE AND THE PRACTICE OF THE ART, RESPECTED BY ALL MEN, IN ALL TIMES BUT SHOULD I TRESPASS AND VIOLATE THIS OATH, MAY THE RESERVE BE MY LOT

Translated by Francis Adams.

limited in the medical field, but had already formulated (2,200 years before Tain and Boll) the theory on *geographical environment's influence* on the temper of nations (theory of geographical determinism). Hippocrates concluded that only the political regime exercised such an influence so as to reverse geographical environment's action. His extremely democratic ideas are mentioned in his treatise **«On Airs, Waters and Places»** where he assails despotic power, that weakens and destroys the ethical and inward substance of citizens.

His whole philosophical point of view had made him a man of deep ethical substance, humble and not fond of money so that he used to offer his services for free to many people and his knowledge to a number of pupils who worthy succeeded him such as his sons *Thessalus* and *Dracon,* his son-in- law *Polyvos, Proxagoras, Kritodimos* (doctor of Alexander the Great), *Dracon* the 2nd, *Dexippos, Herisistratos* (all of them, doctors of Alexander's successors).

His ethics were so great that he established the ethic code of medical profession which clearly determines the mission and duties of doctors and compelled his pupils to swear this code before practicing medicine. This oath is used even today when students graduate in medicine.

Headless statue of Asclepius who is offering an egg to a serpent. Telesphoros-demon is lying by his feet (Archeological Museum of Kos).

He spent his last years in Larissa, Thessaly. Some travelers and many others *(Soranus of Ephessos, Anthimos Gazis,* etc.) claimed that they had seen his grave as well as the grave stone up until 1807, in the area today called Giannouli, around ten minutes off the town. Yet, later on (Turkish occupation era), traces have been lost.

KOS CURRENT FEATURES

An island which had been continuously inhabited since very ancient times has definitely been influenced a lot in the formation of mentality of inhabitants, habits and the island's spirituality or even in its architecture. Traces left by every civilization who evolved either by auto-chthons, either by conquerors are obvious everywhere. Besides, the island is an immense archeological site full of Classical, Hellenistic, Roman, Knight, Turkish and Italian monuments where the researcher of every period can find an intense interest. The simple visitor too, can be charmed by attractive images that their existence in the Aegean scenery and the bright light can offer.

Ancient white marbles which cut the clear blue sky, imposing castles near the blue sea, a fine mosque which gives the island an oriental character, beautiful buildings of the Italian ruling period next to palm trees and current picturesque houses of the locals with vivid island colors, mostly in Mediterranean countries, make a picture where the past mixes with the present and captivates visitors. All this combined with endless beaches, crystal clear water of the Aegean Sea and the marvelous climate have made the island a continuous tourist pole. Kos is now placed among the most cosmopolitan islands in the Mediterranean Sea having quite considerable tourist facilities and an intense night-life. A number of restaurants, taverns, night-clubs, fancy bars, mostly in Kazouli

A windmill in Antimacheia.

Night view to Akti Miaouli Street.

square, and Averof Street, but also numerous cultural events and concerts, which take place mostly during the summer, offer a multi-fold entertainment that can satisfy every taste and desire. Unfortunately, as the exception makes the rule, the skyrocketing and rapid development in tourism has altered the island's character. Huge tourist units, fast-

foods, processed massive entertainment offered to tourist groups certainly deprive the island from its picturesque features and its natural beauty.

Although the locals have given up their traditional occupations and are now working in the tourist sector, they have not stopped preserving their customs and habits. In villages located in Dikaios mount, you will see Koans gathering in cafes to drink some ouzo, eat chick-pea balls and octopus, enjoying simple talking and celebrating their saints with big fairs. Virgin Mary, the Lady of the Aegean Sea, is celebrated in a unique way on August 15. In these villages you can taste the local cuisine and the famous red wine as well as cheese immerged in wine, stuffed lamb, the traditional dish of weddings (beef with small pies). You

can also buy pure and savory thyme honey.

We are going to help you be acquainted with the island as thoroughly as possible starting from archeological sites, then continuing with the rest of the monuments in the historical center of Kos, close trips, as well as three suggested routes in all the island. May our wishes follow your route in this special part of the Earth.

Life goes on slowly at the villages' cafes.

650

Although the rapid development in tourism has altered the island's and the inhabitants' characters, you will see everywhere images of a passed era.

A MAP OF THE TOWN

1. Excavations in the port area. 2. Thermae of the west area. 3. Thermae in the port area. 4. National Bank of Greece. 5. Bus station. 6. Museum. 7. Credit Bank of Greece. 8. Commercial Bank of Greece. 9. Deftedar Mosque. 10. Taxi stand. 11. The plane tree of Hippocrates. 12. Police Station. 13. Courthouse. 14. Chatzi Hasan Mosque. 15. Hospital. 16. Saint Nicolas church . 17. Telecommunications Office 18. Post office. 19. The market. 20. Sainte Paraskevi church 21. The temple of Dionysus. 22. Olympic Airways office. 23. Nymphaeum. 24. "Xysto". 25. Ancient Stadium. 26. A Roman residence. 27. Odeum. 28. Town Hall. 29. Port authority office. 30. Catholic Archdiocese. 31. Stadium.

GETTING TO KNOW THE TOWN

ARCHEOLOGICAL SITES

The ancient city of Kos which was founded somewhere between 366 - 365 BC, used to be extremely large. As findings show, mostly those of the archeologist *R. Herzog* and the Koan historian *Zaraftis,* the city had a perimeter of 4km and an advanced irrigating and drain system, strong walls, a particularly good town-planning following Hippodamus' system, temples, public buildings, gymnasiums, odeons, and generally speaking, all elements of a prosperous city. Archeological research has divided excavations findings in four areas.

A) Excavations in the Port area : In the port, you can see parts of the **Ancient Wall** of the 4th century BC, which used to reach the

The two restored columns of the ancient forum.

port and was 6 to 8 m large. There is also a small **temple** probably that of **Hercules** (12.5m x 9m). Near this small temple, fine mosaics of the 3rd century BC have been found. One of them shows Orpheus accompanied by animals while another shows a symposium offered by Hercules and another one, a fisherman. You can also see:

-**The Ancient Forum** of the 4th century BC, a big rectangular building whose surface was 162 m x 82 m. Two columns of this building, which sustain a part of the epistyle, have been restored.

-**The Eastern gallery** of the 4th century, which is probably the most ancient building

having five wonderful restored columns. Here, a small statue of *Marsyas* hanged has been found (Archeological Museum of Kos) who, according to the legend, was punished, as he wanted to compete with *god Apollo* in music.

-**The sanctuary of Pandimos Aphrodite** or Aphrodisio. It is a "twin" sanctuary whose temple was dedicated to Pandimos Aphrodite and the other one to Potnia Aphrodite. Only some drums of marble columns have survived in both sanctuaries.

-The small **Hellenistic sanctuary** of the 2nd century BC, a state-of-the-art sanctuary, which had the shape of a trapeze.

-**The great palaio-Christian basilica**, which

Ruins of Pandimos Aphrodite's sanctuary.

century BC, a wonderful large mosaic of the 2nd century BC has been found. Part of the mosaic represents scenes of fights between men and bulls, bears and wild boars. Another part represents *Apollo* and the *Muses* and another one, *Dionysus,* as well as Pares' judgment who offers the apple of discord to *Aphrodite.*

Opposite of the West Thermae there is also the **«Nympheum»** or «Folica» as the Romans called it. It is a fine building of the 3rd century BC, which had first been considered as the sanctuary of the Nymphs (thereof it was named after them); yet, later on, it has been understood that it was simply a building housing public WCs. Eleven of its columns have been restored, its internal walls are decorated with colorful marbles up to 1.80m, it has a patio decorated with mosaics, while you can see drain installations.

Above: a view of the Nymphaeum interior, a fine building of the 3rd century AD. Left: Odeum, (2nd century AD)

The Odeum. It is a building of the 2nd century BC, which had been built following the shape of ancient theaters. It has been well-preserved and was found in 1929 by the archeologis L Lamvrezi. It is composed of nine series of seats, a large part of it has been restored, while the whole building stands on vaulted chambers according to the Roman model. A number of statues, among which that of Hippocrates (Archeological Museum of Kos) as well as a mosaic representing scenes with birds, have been found there.

East of «Xysto» you can see a restored room of Corinthian order, with a rotunda,where the **Vespacian Therme** used to be during the Roman period. In Via Decumana, one of the paves that goes through the archeological site, there are ruins of ancient residencies with magnificent mosaics. The most important one, is that in

the **residence of the kidnapping of Europe** where the so-called mosaic has been found. The residence had three spacious chambers and many smaller ones, as well as two columns, and a big back-yard. Its toilet is also remarkable where you can still see the drain system. Statues representing *Asclepius, Artemis, Hygeia* (Health) and *resting Hermes*, which are now exhibited in the Archeological museum of Kos have also

The ancient gymnasium, "Xysto". An impressive building of the Hellenistic period with 81 columns, 17 of which have been restored.

been found there as well as some frescos which represent couples of dancers, birds and mythological couples. There is also a fresco which represents a scene with a messenger and bears an inscription on it mentioning «I am running all twelve hours».

The Roman Residence (**Casa Romana**) was discovered in 1933 by the archeologist *L. Lavrenzi.* It dates back to the 3rd century and has been built on the ruins of an older

Hellenistic residence. It is of Pompeian order and has three atriums. In the first atrium, there is a magnificent Hellenistic mosaic of fine art, which represents a deer being attacked by a tiger. In the adjacent chamber, there is a Hellenistic mosaic of an exceptional perfection, which has probably been transferred here and represents scenes of maritime life. The walls in the second atrium are decorated with marbles and the floor around the decorative cistern has a mosaic that represents a Nereid riding a hippocampus and is accompanied by dolphins. The third atrium, which is bigger, is surrounded by two lines of Ionic columns located at all three sides, while at the

southern part, columns are of Corinthian order. The first line rests on the floor while the second one rests on a balcony. A decorative cistern and various mosaics decorate this marvelous place.

Opposite of the Casa Romana, there are ruins of a Hellenistic marble temple and an alter of Dionysus. Ruins of the ancient Stadium (2nd century BC) of 200 m long and 30 m large have also survived. The «aphesis» (starting point), i.e. the point where the starters used to give the signal for a race to start, can also be seen there. Last, at the north-west side of the port there are **the circular Thermae**, a building of the Roman period, which have been named after their circular shape.

G) Central area of excavations :

It is located in the center of the city and is surrounded by 31st Martiou (March) Street, Kolokotroni Street, Peissandros Street and Eleftherias (Liberty) Square. There are not any particularly remarkable ruins, yet there is a considerable number of marvelous mosaics. There are fragments of a Mycenaean settlement, a necropolis of pre-Geometrical age, which contains 77 tombs of children and adults as well as many vessels, which are now exhibited in the Archeological museum of Kos.

"Kidnapping of Europe". This marvelous Hellenistic mosaic gave its name to the residence where it was found.

At the east side of the **«residence of the bronze»** there have been found bronze statuettes of *Artemis, Hares, Demeter* and *Isis.* On a barrow located at the junction of Peisandros Street and Kolokotronis Street there used to be an **ancient Acropolis** where there have been found ruins of a construction with a cistern and two alcoves, parts of the yard and fragments of a mosaic. Near the old mosque there have been found two mosaics of the 3rd century AD with scenes representing leopards and fishes.

ted today. Some parts of the walls, as well as some bulwarks and towers have survived. The most impressive tower is the circular one which is situated at the south-west side of the walls while at the main gate you can see the blazon of the Grand Master, *de Heredia*, and that of the governor of the island, *Schregellholz.*

THE CASTLE

It is located inside the walls, at the entrance of the port so as the city is not seized from the sea. It is surrounded by two yards. One of them is external and has four circular ramparts at each of the four angles and the other one is internal and has four circular towers. It has been built on the ruins of the Ancient and the Byzantine fortifications. This is the reason why you can see many architectural parts built in the walls. The castle is divided into different periods of the Knights' era. It has been repeatedly fortified for defense purposes and was completed in 1514 during the rule of the Grand Master *D'Ambuaz* and governor D*el Caretto.* This is the explanation for a great number of blazons which have been built-in several places, and mostly on gates.

The main entrance is from the bridge which is perpendicular to the *Palm trees avenue.* It used to have three vaulted bridges and a roving bridge so as to be secured while the main gate used to be surrounded by marble pilasters and three blazons at the transom. The whole castle has been preserved at a very good state and its accessibility makes it possible for everyone to go around and enjoy its magnificent view. At the internal side of the castle a number of architectural parts of ancient and Hellenistic temples, pillars, inscriptions, capitals and altars have been preserved.

ARCHEOLOGICAL MUSEAM

At the north side of the *Eleftherias Square*, opposite of the building of the *Municipal Market* lies the **Archeological Museum**. It is a two-floored building which was built during the Italian ruling period. It has an impressive gate, an imi-tation of Roman Thermae, and consists of a hall, a rotunda and three chambers in the ground-floor and one floor. It mostly houses findings of the Hellenistic and the Roman periods but also marvelous Early Christian mosaics.

Exhibited items at the Hall : Circular and rectangular tomb-stones of the Hellenistic era beautifully decorated such

Below: next to Deftedar Mosque, the two-floored Archeological Museum is situated. Right: A group composed of god Dionysus, Pan and a Satyr. Erotideas is playing with a panther by their feet.

as heads of oxes, the *corn of Amaltheia*, etc. Also, a Roman relief representing a horse's head, another one representing a figure of a lion which used to be built-in the castle of the Knights, a marble frog-part of a fountain's decoration - as well as colossal heads of *goddess Demeter* and another one, pro-bably that of *Agrippine*, all made in the 1st century AD.

Exhibited items in the Rotunda: At the center of the floor, there is a wonderful mosaic (2nd or 3rd century AD), which represents Asclepius' s arrival in the island while he is welcomed by a Koan and Hippocrates who sits beside a rock. There is also a very beautiful statuette of a child who holds a goose, that dates back to the Hellenistic era, various tomb-stone reliefs, among which prevails one of the 2nd century BC, which represents a dead man on a ship being proclaimed hero and headless statues of women and Muses bearing marks of pigments (2nd century BC).

In the Rotunda, statues are exhibited which have been found in the residence with the mosaic of «Kidnapping of Europe» as well as that of *Hygeia* (Health) who holds a snake and offers it an egg while *Eros* and *Ypnos* (Sleep) are repre-sented at her feet (2nd century BC), the headless statue of *Asclepius* with *Tele-sphoros-Demon* at his feet (2nd century BC), the complex of god *Dionysus* and *Pan* and a satyr while *Eros* plays at his feet with an animal, as well as relief pendetives of tables decorated with scenes of god *Dionysus* and a *Grypas* (a mythical animal with lion body and eagle head and wings).

Eastern room : There are exhibits of Roman period. There are also headless statues of *Ephesian Artemis*, seated *De-*

The statue of goddess Hygeia -Health (2nd century AD), holding a serpent whom she is offering an egg to. Eros-Ypnos is lying on her feet. It has been found in the residence of "Kidnapping of Europe".

Left: a statue of a young woman of the Trajanus' era. It has been found in the residence of Europe.
Above-right: a statue of a woman of the Roman period; it has been found in Odeum area.
Above: A head of Hermes of the Roman period.
Right: a small statue of a young satyr found in the Roman residence, (Late Hellenistic era).

meter and dressed women, bodies of *Hygeia,* a naked woman and a man and the wonderful statue of *Hermes* who wears a petasos (hat) and sandals, holds a cadeceus (Kyrikeion) and is seated on a rock. There are also heads of Roman emperors such as *Trajanus* and *Antoninus the Pius* and other heads among which that of *Perseus* , the only one dating back to the Hellenistic period. There is also a table with lion legs and an abutment decorated with *Marsyas* hanged.

Western room : There are findings of Archaic and Hellenistic era. You will notice statues of *Victory, Hippocrates,* a colossal head of *Hercules,* which is a variation of a work made by the sculptor *Lysippus,* a head of *Alexander the Great* as well as two reliefs one of which represents a scene of a symposium of the 6th century BC and another one representing a child holding a cock.

Northern room : There are exhibits, mostly of the Hellenistic period among which you can see: the statue of goddess *Aphrodite* armed, *Tyche* (Hazard) (1st century AD), Muse *Clio, Athena, Demeter Melagris* and *Demeter Lycourgis, Persephone* (daughter) of the 4th century BC. There are also various statues of *Aphrodite, Demeter, Hermaphrodite, Persephone,* as well as a replica of the great sculptor *Praxiteles* and heads of *Selinos, Aphrodite* and *Hermes,* a part of a Hermaic stele of the 1st century BC, a relief re-presenting Her-cules shooting Stymfalides birds with a bow and a complex of youngsters represented playing «Ephedrismos» (1st century BC). At the first floor of the museum, there are ceramics of different periods, vessels as well as architectural parts of temples.

Hermes with a small goat. A work made in the 2nd century AD, which has been found in the residence of "Kidnapping of Europe".

OTHER SIGHTSEEING IN THE TOWN

Opposite of the entrance of the castle, there is a square where a historic tree dominates. It is the **plane-tree of Hippocrates**. According to tradition, *Hippocrates* used to teach under that 2,500 year-old tree. Its diameter is almost 12 meters and as a conseguence this very ancient tree has been associated with many legends and traditions. Next to the protective grating, a Hellenistic sarcophagi had been placed since the Turkish occupation era, which has been transformed into a fountain so as

the close Logia could be irrigated. On top of it, there is an Arab inscription mentioning the year of the mosque's founding. A little further, you can see a beautiful two-floor majestic building with a fine mosque. It is a **mosque of Gazi Hassan pasha**, also called Loggia, which was built in 1788 of architectural parts from the ancient city.

At the end of the charming **Palm trees Street** that passes through the gate of the castle and near the plane tree of Hippocrates, there is **Akti Miaouli Street** on the right. You can see there, some of the most interesting buildings, as far as architecture is concerned, those of Italian ruling period,

The plane tree of Hippocrates. According to tradition, he used to teach his students under the shadow of that tree.

which have been built according to the same peculiar order as those in Rhodes. The most important ones are the **Dioikitirion** (Administration Center) with its characteristic clock and the Archdiocese and the Cathedral.

At the central **Eleftheria Square**, you

Eleftheria square. On the left, the Municipal Market and on the right, Deftedar Mosque.

will see peculiar buildings such as the **Municipal Market** , the Club, the Taxes Gate and the **Archeological Museum**. They all have been built during the Italian ruling period. You will also see the **Deftedar mosque** a building of the Turkish ruling period.

Left: the Administration Center (Dioikitirion) with its characteristic clock.
Below: the Tax Gate.
Right: Loggia, built in 1786 from constructing materials of the ancient city.

PLATANOS
RESTAURANT
CAFE BAR

ROUTES IN KOS ISLAND

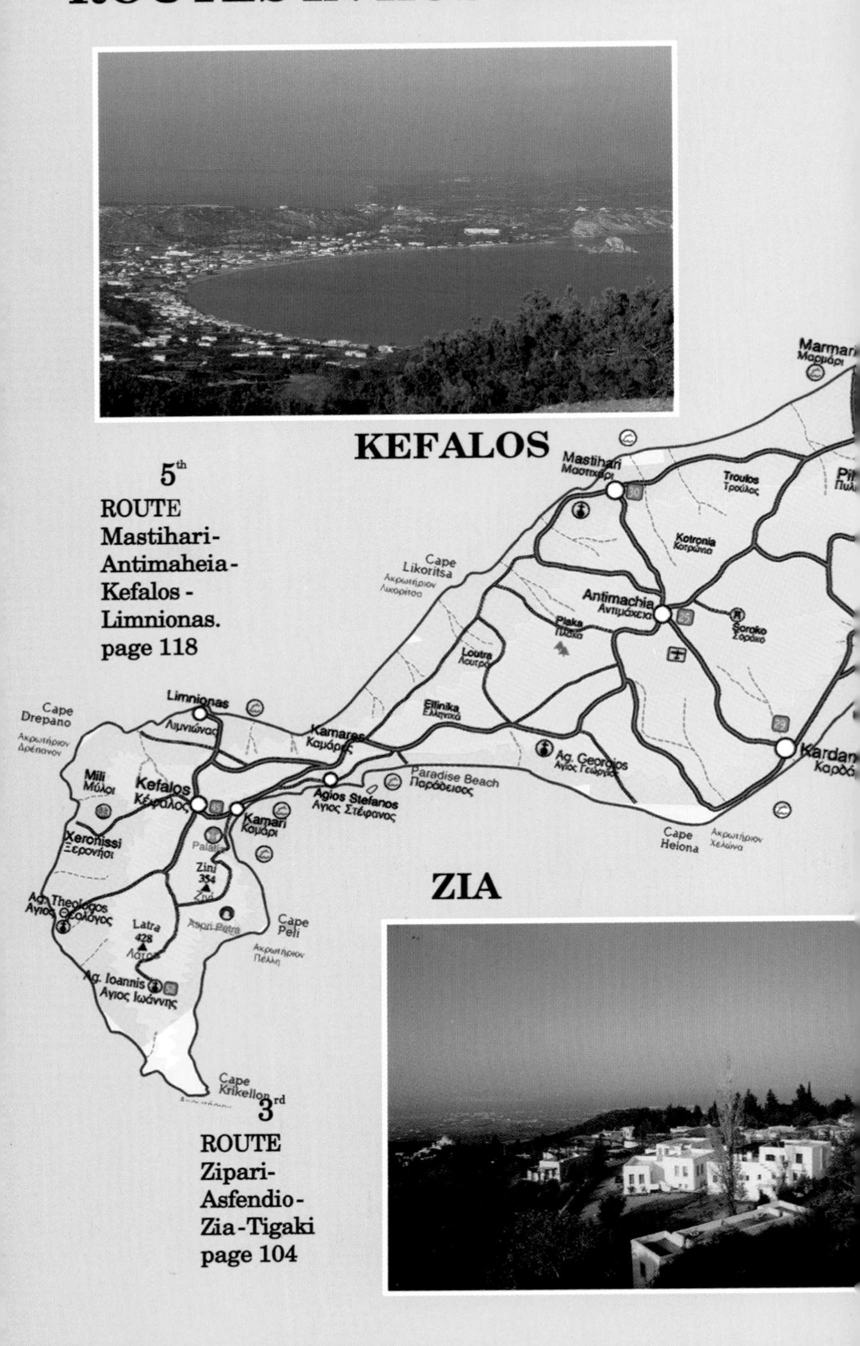

1st
ROUTE
Platani - Asclepium
page 92

ASCLEPIUM

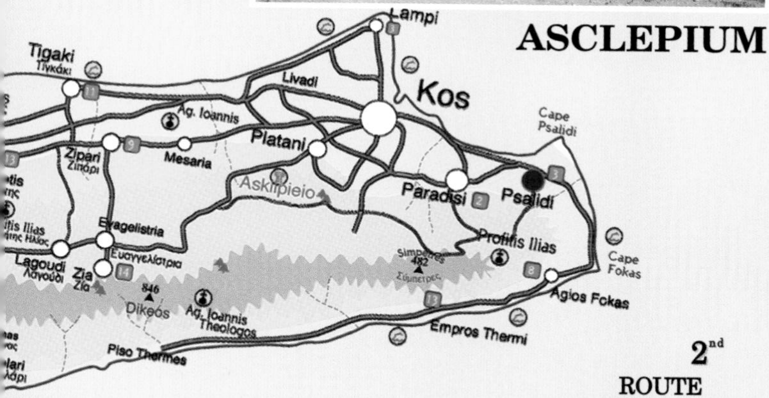

2nd
ROUTE
Paradisi - Psalidi - Aghios Fokas - Thermae.
page 102

4th
ROUTE
Linopotis - Pyli - Kardamaina
page 110

THERMA

KARDAMENA

1ST ROUTE

KOS - PLATANI - ASCLEPIUM

Should you head south-west of Asclepium, you will meet **Platani**, also known as *Kermetes,* which is now part of the town and is located 2 km off. It is an area where the few Turkish inhabitants of the island used to live. It is a picturesque village with a particular and popular architecture influenced by the Muslim inhabitants. There are also traditional cafes as well as a mosque which is still in service. Close to the village's square, there are ruins of a big Roman tomb.

ASCLEPIUM

On a green hill, just 4 km off the town, there is the famous **Asclepium**, the most important archeological monument in the island. Asclepiums used to be sanctuaries for god Asclepius where «Asclepiads» (physicians) used to practice medicine. Out of 300

Asclepiums in the Greek area, the most well-known ones have been those of *Trikkis* (Trikala) in Thessaly where the worship of the god was born, that of Epidaurus, Amphiareio, and that of Kos.

The most important Asclepium has been probably that of Kos, since the famous Hippocrates, founder of the medical science had taught and established the first medical school there. It was discovered in 1902, during the Turkish occupation period, by the German archeologist *Rudolf Hergoz* on the instructions of the Koan historian and researcher *Jacob Zaftaris*. Unfortunately, a large part of the findings has been transferred to Constantinople and mainly to Berlin. The Asclepium was composed of three levels (andera) and was surrounded by a sacred forest, where - according to *Pausanias* - it was forbidden for someone to be born or die.

Left: the 7 restored columns in Apollo's temple. Below: part of the fortified walls between the first and the second level (anderum)

A staircase of 24 stairs that leads you to **Propylaea** takes you to the first level (anderum), which used to have a gallery formed by all its three sides. Behind the gallery, there used to be a series of chambers whose foundations can still be seen today. In

10
9
C
8
7
B
2
4
6
A
5
1
3

Representation of Asclepium according to the archeologist R. Herzog:
A: first level. B: second level. C: third level. 1. Propylaea. 2. Spa chambers. 3. Rooms for patients. 4. Fortification wall with niches. 5. Asclepius' temple. 6. Chambers for priests. 7. Asclepius' halter. 8. Apollo's temple. 9. Asclepius' larger temple. 10. Rooms for patients.

this building complex, there used to be the medical school, an anatomy and pathology museum as well as rooms for patients. In the two underground chambers (chambers of Aphrodisiacs) a temple of *Aphrodite* is believed to have existed which was decorated with the famous statue of the goddess made by *Praxiteles*. Many statuettes have been found there which represent various phases of diseases or sick parts of the body.

At the southern part of the anderum you can see an abutment wall with spas. A scene, representing god Pan who holds a flute under his feet where a spring is running through, has survived in a niche at the left of the staircase. Out of the perimeter of the anderum there are ruins of Roman thermae. A staircase of 30 stairs leads you to the second anderum. At the left of the staircase there is an inscription from a small temple of the great Koan physician, *Gaius Stertinius Xenophon*, personal doctor of the Roman emperor *Claudius*. At the center of the anderum there used to be the oldest edifice of the whole complex, the halter of Kyparissios Apollo (4th century BC) of which some fragments have survived. You can see two restored columns from the **temple of *Apollo*** of the 3rd century BC, of Ionian order and its altar. Around it, there used to be a small gallery and near that some statues of *Asclepium, Hygeia* and *Apione*, made by *Kifissodotos* and *Timachus*, both sons of Praxiteles. Behind the temple, there used to be chambers for priests as well as the «Abaton» (impassable) and the spring of the «sacred water». The most impressive of all findings is the **temple of Apollo**, with columns on its sides, of Corinthian order probably built in the 2nd century BC. Only 7 columns have been restored. You can also see ruins of the Club, a semi-circular podium from a Hellenistic edifice as well as a small temple

Below: Aerial view to Asclepium where the first two levels can be seen.

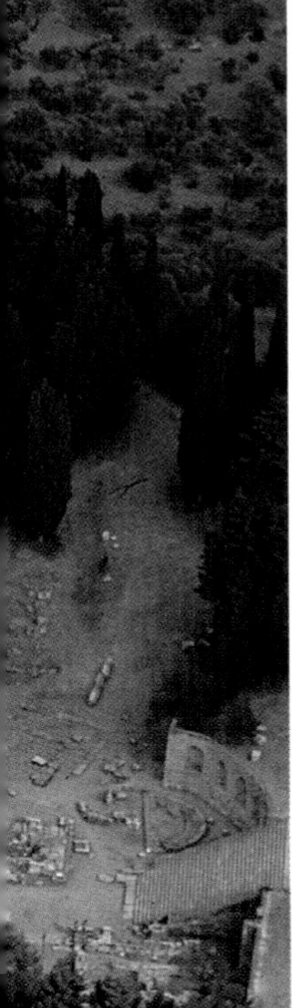

dedicated to *Nero* and ruins of a staircase that used to lead to the «sacred forest» which surrounded Asclepium.

A third staircase which is cut in-between and bears 60 stairs leads you to the third anderum (80m x 100m) where the great **temple of Asclepius** (2nd century BC) used to dominate. Is was of Doric order with columns on its sides, measuring 34 m x 18 m and containing 104 columns. You can see ruins of a Hellenistic gallery which used to surround the anderum from all three sides and where there used to be rooms for patients. On the same level, you can see traces of a small temple of the 5th century BC, probably that of *Apollo* as well as fragments of a staircase which used to lead to the sacred forest.

A representation of Hippocrates' Oath takes place every Sunday in the summer, in every area of the Asclepium.

THE INTERNATIONAL INSTITUTE OF HIPPOCRATES

Near the Asclepium, on an area of 24 hectares there are facilities of the Hippocratic International Institute of Kos, which was founded on October 29, 1960. Today, delegations of more than 60 countries are members of it. The aims of the Institute consist in promoting and publicly acknowledging medical research, publishing medical treatises and the works of Hippocrates and all manuscripts related with medical science.

A number of scientists of international prestige often visit the Institute and make their announcements. In the future, a modern «city of Hippocrates» is going to be created where an international medical Olympiad will take place every 4 or 5 years.

2ND ROUTE

PSALIDI - AGHIOS FOKAS - THERMAE

As you leave the town, you will head east and you will pass from **Paradissi** (2 km off) and **Psalidi** (3 km off), villages with well-organized beaches, camping sites, etc. 8 km further you will reach the marvelous, clear **beach of Aghios Fokas**. It is an extremely tourist beach with hotels, restaurants, night-clubs, etc. Ruins of a three-aisled Palaio-Christian basilica have been found in the greater area. It was dedicated to Saint Gabriel. There are also ruins of a Roman villa (near Dimitra Hotel) as well as ruins of Pelasgian walls.

13 km off the town, you will meet **Thermae**, a wonderful beach and spas with organized facilities. Water in theses spas are indicated for rheumatics, arthritis, and gynecological diseases. North of the town, you will reach nice and well-organized beaches. In the area of **Lampi** (3 km off) some old windmills have still survived which make for a special local character. Lampi is famous for its wonderful, yet, very tourist beaches.

Right: mineral springs' outfall, Thermae. Below: Aerial view to Psalidi.

3RD ROUTE

ZIPARI-ASFENDIO-ZIA-TIGAKI

As you leave the town and head north-west, you will meet a mountainous village, called **Zipari** 9 km off. It is a newer village where you should take interest in visiting a big church complex, the **basilica of Saint Paul's**. It dates back to the first period of the Christian era and measures 21.60m x 15m. Parts of foundations and walls of a cross-shaped baptistery have survived. A little further, an equally remarkable basilica of 17 m x 16.30 m has been found which bears interesting mosaics, a circular baptistery and a dome. Near the village, there is also the chapel of Saint John of Chostos (16th century AD).

As you continue, you reach the foot of Dikaios Mount.You will soon reach its most picturesque village in Kos, **Asfendio** (14 km off). It is built among the green, fresh, high slope where clear water runs through and where an amazing view to

Right: Pictures from the marvelous communities of Asfendio. Below: "Panayia sto Langadi" (Virgin Mary in the valley).

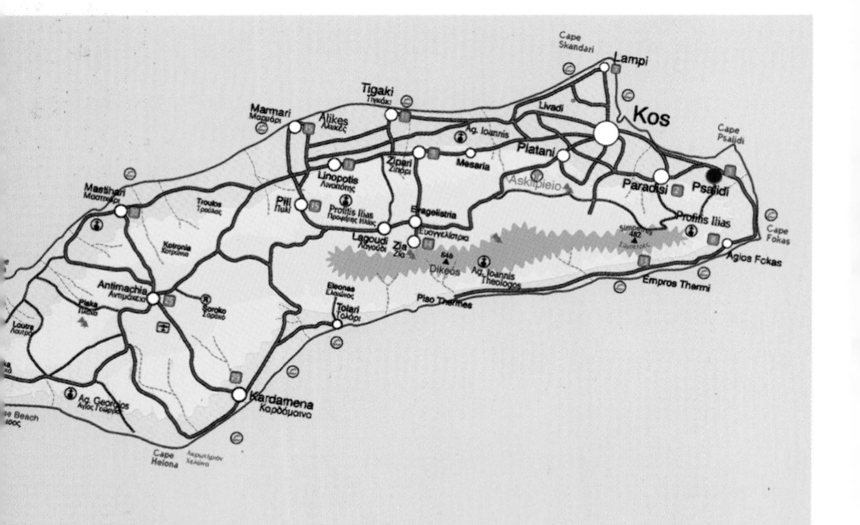

the Asia Minor coasts gives you an original sense of peace. The village is composed of five scattered communities: **Evangelistria** at the center of which there is a big modern church, **Asomatos** and its church along with its temple of the 11th century named after the community. **Zia**, the beautiful, traditionally preserved and green village with its amazing view, has been proclaimed protected community due to its special beauty. Very close to Zia you can see the small «Moni ton Spondon»

The wonderful and all-green Zia built at the slopes of Dikaios mount.

(monastery of libations) of the 11th century which was probably built by Saint Christodoulos around 1086. It is of classic Byzantine order while only the small temple of Virgin Mary has survived. At the place called Kafalovrysi, you can see the monastery dependency and its chapel where water is running through. On November 21, a celebration takes place. You will also see «Panayia Kyparisiotisa» a beautiful chapel as well as several and more recent monasteries celebrating their patron saints in summertime. On a hill, you will see the small Byzantine church of Dikaios Christos, built in 1079 AD with an imperial golden bull and a remarkable temple. The whole Zia and Asfendios communities and a number of post-Byzantine churches are now protected areas of cultural tradition. The communities of **Aghios Dimitrios** (Haihoutes) which is now deserted and **Lagoudi** along with its church, Aghios Ioannis Theologos ton Vrachon, also belong to this category.

North, 6.5 km off Asfendio, you will meet the seaside resort of **Tigaki**, a wonderful sandy and green beach which is a very tourist place. At the place called Voukolia you will see ruins of an old Christian church, while the island, which can be seen opposite is the very beautiful and peaceful Pserimos. You can visit it by small shuttle boats.

The church of Assumption, the only edifice that has survived from the "Monastery of Libations" of the 11th century AD.

Below: the sandy beach in the very tourist place, Tigaki

4TH ROUTE

LINOPOTIS-PILI-KARDAMAINA

You should first start with this nice route from Zipari and if you continue you will meet 13 km off, the special village called **Linopotis**. It is a village which was created in 1925 by a colonization of Italians during the Italian rule period. Here, you will see a big source which ends up to an artificial lake that irrigates the whole plain of the area. In this very same area, ruins of an ancient villa, a Roman aqueduct, and those of a Palaio-Christian basilica have been found. If you head north you will see **Marmari** 3 km further, an endless beach of 2 km long, very developed as far as tourism is concerned with big hotel units and a good infrastructure.

Then, you follow the way to **Pyli** (15 km off), a village composed of three communities with a history of a great economic prosperity mostly thanks to

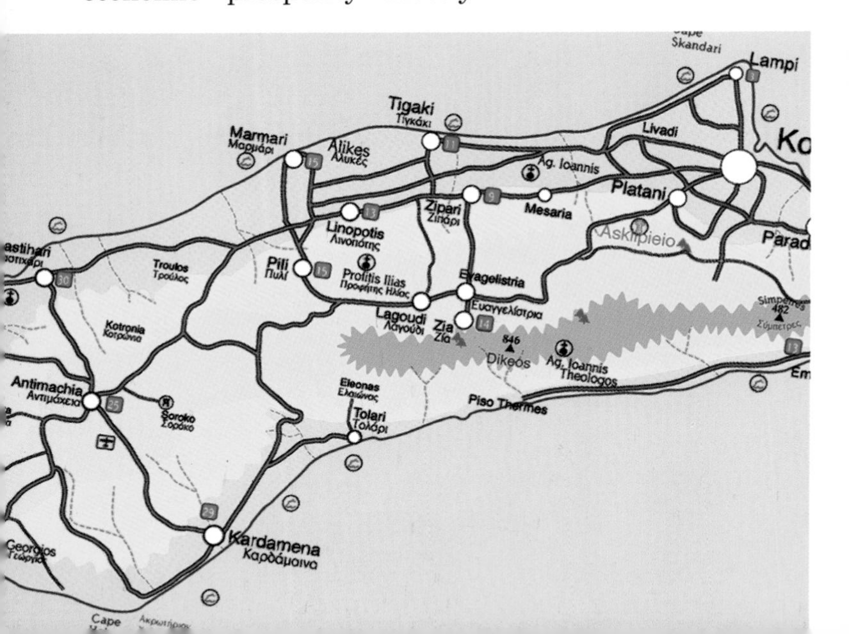

Right: a scarecrow to protect vegetables. "Artistic" expression in Pyli. Below: the beach in Marmari, a place where tourism has been very developed.

tomato production. At the community of Aghios Nikolaos, ruins of the tomb of Charmylos, a hero of ancient Kos, as well as the source which has been named after him, have still survived. Charmylos' tomb was renovated in 1592 and is decorated with six fountains. Very close, you will see ruins of Knight buildings. In the Konario neighbor, a Palaio-Christian basilica of Saint Basil has been found. A little higher, at the place of the old Pyli you can see ruins of a Byzantine castle as well as a **monastery**

Kardamaina, probably the most tourist place on the island.

of Ypapantis Theotokou (Kastrianon) built by Saint Christodoulos in the 11th century (around 1085). It contains a marble credence, which rests on 4 columns as well as fragments of hagiographies. On April 23, at the neighbor of Aghios Georgios a fair takes place, horse races are organized and food and wine are offered.

As you head south you reach **Kardamaina** (29 km) where its beautiful beach is 6 km long and maybe the most tourist and highly cosmopolitan area on the island. On a hill off

the village you will see ruins of a **castle of Saint John's Knights.** On its façade there is an inscription that informs you on the date the castle was built: 1494.

In that area there used to be the ancient city of Alassarna, bigger than today's one. The big temple of god Apollo, the foundations of which have been found, used to be located there. The temple was the most ancient and the second in wealth on the island after Asclepium. Also, ruins of ancient edifices, an ancient theater as well as a Hellenistic and a Roman one and the foundations of a big Palaio-Christian basilica of «Aghia Theotitos» (Sainte Divinity) as well as three other dating back to the same period, have been found there. Kardamaina used to have a great tradition in pottery that has now declined. Nevertheless, you can find nice hand-made ceramics at the unique workshop. Small boats leave from Kardamaina to Nisyros.

Aerial view to Kardamaina.

The wonderful beach of Kardamaina, which is more than 6 km long.

5TH ROUTE

MASTIHARI - ANTIMAHEIA - KEFALOS - AGHIOS STEFANOS – KAMARI - SAINT JOHN'S MONASTERY

Some kilometers off Linopotis, you can head north and at the 30th km you will reach Mastihari, a seaside village with amazing beaches. **Mastihari** was set up after the earthquake of 1933 when people of Antimaheia took refuge there. There are also an intense tourist development and many facilities. At the wonderful beach of Aghios Ioannis (Saint John) there are ruins of a special - by Oriental and African standards - three-aisled Palaio-Christian **basilica of Saint John** (5th century AD) with a remarkable baptistery and mosaic floors. Boats leave daily for Kalymnos

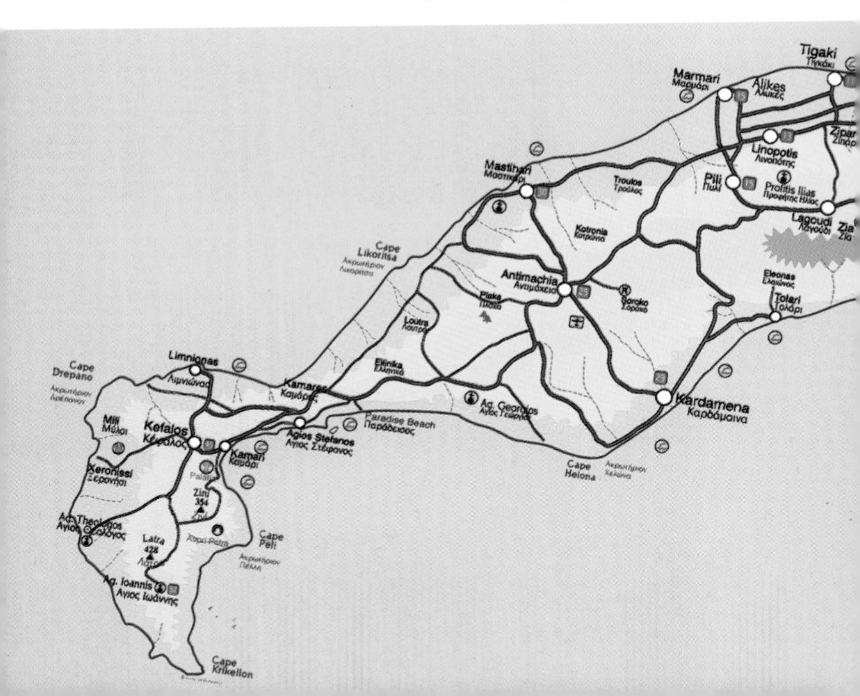

from the small port.

4 km off Mastihari you will meet **Antimaheia** (25 km). During this route you can see Saint George's chapel with various built-in ancient architectural parts. The various ancient findings prove that the ancient demos of Antimaheia and a little further the demos of Asgelis with a great temple of Hera, used to be there. Antimaheia is a Mediterranean traditional village populated by joyful people who adore drinking good wine and dancing as proven by the fairs they organize. It is interesting visiting the Antimaheian house where there is a popular representation of a traditional house of the early 20th century. On a hill, 3 km off the village on the east, there is a well -preserved **Venetian castle** that has been built on ruins of an older fortification wall. You can clearly see warehouses, cisterns, gates, various

Aerial view to the village and the beaches of Mastichari.

chambers, etc. Inside the castle two churches are located, that of Sainte Paraskevi - a single-aisled basilica where a fair takes place on July 26, and ruins of Saint Nicolas' church on the lintel of which you can see a built-in table, Knights' blazons and the date 1520. At the gate of the castle you can see the blazon of the great Magistrate D'Aubuson and the date 1494. Kos airport is located in this area.

Now, go to Kefalos village. At a short distance off Antimaheia, you can take a fresh rest at the place called **Plaka** where vegetation and abundant water create a wonderful scenery which has been nicely transformed into a rest

area. Many peacocks make the scenery even more beautiful. As you keep on, you will reach a beautiful beach, **Paradisos** (Paradise), which is located just a short way off Kefalos bay. Crystal clear wa-ters and the amazing beach are very popular and much-frequented.

After Tigani peninsula you will meet a junction where the right road takes you to **Aghios Stefanos** while the left one takes you up to Kefalos. There, you will enjoy one of the most beautiful beaches on the island. It is worth noticing ruins of two twin Early-Christian three-aisled basilicas (469 and 554 AD) with a common baptistery and marvelous mosaics. They were found

The very well preserved Venetian castle in Antimacheia.

and restored in 1932 by the Italian archeologist L. Lorenzi. Opposite of them, you will see an impressive islet, Kastri where there is a small monastery of Saint Antonios.

As you continue your trip by the sea, you will reach 1.5km further a picturesque small port, **Kamari**. Here, you will see ruins and parts of an ancient seaport of ancient Astypalaia. This large beach is very tourist and has a good infrastructure such as hotels, organized beaches, sea sports, night-clubs, Club Med facilities, etc.

The inland road of the intersection takes you to **Kefalos** (45 km), an all-green village built on an amphitheatric place on a porous hill at the peak of which you can see the picturesque Papavasilis windmill. Here, at the place called Palatia you will see ruins of the ancient city of the island, **Astypalaia**, which was destroyed by an earthquake in 412 BC. A small Asclepium of classic era and ruins of a Hellenistic theatre (2nd century BC), a temple of Doric order dedicated to goddess Demeter, the headless statue of Muse Clio as well as traces of other temples, all dating back to Hellenistic era, have been found there. A giant head of Hercules and a headless statue of goddess Demeter which have been found in this area are exhibited in the Archelogical Museum of Kos. In the same area you will see the small chapel of Panayia Palatiani which has been built on a part of a more ancient temple of god Dionysus and on the more recent temple of goddess Demeter, of Doric order. In fact, the ancient demos of Isthmiotes used to be located there. On a hill, next to the

The beach "Paradisos" (Paradise), probably the most beautiful one on the island.

village you will see ruins of a Venetian castle which has been fortified by Saint John's Knights and later by the Turks.

From Kefalos you will continue south to Zini mount where the prehistoric cave of **«Aspri Petra»** is located that contains findings of Neolithic Age. 7 km further, you will reach Saint John's monastery built on a slope of the mountain inside a charming green scenery. A fair takes place on August 29. If you

Kefalos bay.

head north of Kefalos you will reach a protected natural bay, **Limnionas,** a wonderful shelter from the winds of the Aegean Sea. This is the end of our guiding. Still, you will be able to discover untouched beauties and virgin beaches, either on foot or by boat.

Right and left: "Waves" on the sand of Paradisos beach. Below: Opposite of the beach of Aghios Stefanos lies Kastri, a small islet.

NISYROS

... of lave and waves

A piece of lave at the edge of the Sea roughed by the salt of the waves has created this island of a rare and amazing beauty. The volcano, creator of this intense scenery, has drawn images which hit your senses in an unfamiliar way. The area is harsh and hard, that's why whoever is captured by it they will never cease being amazed by this special beauty.

GEOGRAPHY AND MORPHOLOGY

Nisyros is a small volcanic island lying between Kos and Tilos. Its area is 415 km and its coastline 28 km. It is located 200 nautical miles off Piraeus and just 8 nautical miles off Kos, where you can visit it from.

The largest part of the island is mountainous with rocks of volcanic structure that have been created from the volcano, which dates back to very ancient times. The island has a fertile ground and an extremely rich flora. The caldera of the -now inactive- volcano (the last explosion dated back to 1888 AD) is 698 m high, has a diameter of 260 m and a deep of 30 m. It is the major attraction pole on the island. As a consequence of the island's geomorphology, there are layers of hot spas

The volcano whose action has been known since ancient times is the creator of an "intense landscape" in Nisyros island.

which spring as well as a number of exploitable mineral rocks, such as pumice stone.

MYTHOLOGY - HISTORY

The creation of Nisyros is related with the myth of Polyvotis the Giant and his battle against god Poseidon during

Gigantomachy. After his defeat, the Giant, persecuted by Poseidon, tried to take refuge to Kos. Poseidon threw a trident against him and cut a piece from the island that he threw over Polyvotis and buried him under. That's how Nisyros was created while Polyvotis' roars coming from the depths have been associated with those of the volcano.

The caldera of the inactive, still not extinct, volcano.

This tradition shows the island's special bonds with Kos which have been proven by many ancient inscriptions. In Kos, there also was a community of people of Nisyros, called Nisyriadae. Bonds that were associating the two islands were cultural, social, economic and political (common power, alliances, etc.)

As proven by findings, Nisyros had already been populated in prehistoric period (Neolithic Age). Homer mentioned that Nisyros had taken part in the Trojan War. The island was probably inhabited by

Simple white houses with flat roofs will impress you, in Mandraki, the capital of the island.

Dorics in historic times and later on became member of the Athenian Alliance. As far as classical period is concerned, Palaiocastro - an Acropolis located in the ancient city - has survived. In 200 BC, the island was annexed to the sovereignty of Rhodes. Over the next years, Nisyros has been following the fate of all Dodecanese Islands. Thus, Byzantines made their presence obvious through many churches they built during that period. Saint John's Knights left their marks, too, with this castle. Turks and Italians have exercised

less influence. The island was liberated and united with Greece in 1948 like the rest of the Dodecanese Islands.

GETTING TO KNOW THE ISLAND

Should you access the island by sea you will be generously rewarded by a wonderful and impressive picture made by the white color of houses, coupled with orange-like ground and the blue color of the Aegean Sea. The grace of Nisyros, which is due to the mystical character and to a sense of peace it offers, captures visitors - mostly those seeking for something different, something not cosmopolitan; since Nisyros is far from being a cosmopolitan island but a special one.

Mandraki which is both a port and the island's capital, impresses you with the beauty of the simplicity of white houses, flat roofs, reed roofs, multicolored frames of windows and doors and flowered yards decorated with geraniums and wonderful bougainvilleas. Its narrow streets go up to the rock at the peak of which lies the **Knights' castle** built by Saint John's Knights (1315), which is preserved at a good state. Inside the castle, there is the **monastery of Panagia tis Spilianis** (Virgin Mary of the Cave) - built around 1600 AD - and rich in offerings, made by religious people, and in ecclesiastic jewels. There is also a rich library where one can find remarkable manuscripts as well as rare editions. The catholic is a basilica with a temple of the 18th century. Next, there is a chapel dedicated to Saint Charalampos. On August 15, on the name-day of the monastery's saint patron a two-day fair takes place during which good domestic wine is offered. Northwest, over

Mandraki, lies Palaiocastro where parts of a fortified yard of the 4th century and ruins of the ancient city have been found. There is also an ancient cemetery with findings of the 7th and 6th centuries BC and a tomb of the 5th century BC. At the central square of the port, coffee and the famous local drink «soumada» served in small pic-turesque cafes are things you can really enjoy while time seems to forget you. Life goes on at a different, slow, calm pace, journals never arrive on time, and talking with the locals, eating fresh octopus, liastes tomates (sun-berried tomates), sakouliasti (local cheese) become the essence of happiness. It would be worth spending some time at the historic

Paloi, the old port of the island.

Popular art Museum while 1 km off the village there are spas for therapeutic purposes. A small road behind the castle leads you to **Hohlakia**, a particular beach with big black volcanic flat shingles.

Northeast of Mandraki, and as soon as you pass off **Loutra** and its spas (already known since Hippocrates times), the seaside road takes you to a small fishery village, **Paloi**, an old port on the island

The picturesque Emporeio village.

where you can find today small picturesque taverns serving fresh fish. You can have a swim at the large beach of black sand or, should you decide to walk for ten minutes, you will reach the amazing beach of **Aghia Irini** (Sainte Irene). At Lyes you will find a few visitors and crystal clear waters.

3 km off Palous, the uphill road leads you to the small inland village called **Emporeio** (9 km) which is located in lush vegetation

of citrus trees. At the highest place on the island, ruins of another Venetian castle have been found, inside whom there is a Byzantine church of Taxiarchis with excellent hagiography. At a short distance, the **monastery of Panayias Kyras** (Pigis Kyras) stands taller and lonesome opposite of an amazing view. It is an interesting place from an historical point of view. A celebration takes place there during a great fair on August 23.

As you continue heading south by the inland road, you will meat the almost remote **Nikia.** There are new, well-shaped houses, still, without people. They are houses built by people who had migrated abroad and have returned back with money to rebuild their village. Thus, the place revives only in the summer when they come back. At the shingle-paved square, you can sit at a small tavern, opposite of the Aegean Sea, where you can enjoy simple and pure snacks. Beside you, you will see the small church of Theologos which is celebrated on September 26. From here, you can reach **Lakki plateau** where there is also the inactive, yet not extinct, volcano. You will have a strong sense of a lunar scenery and a smell of sulfur and Polyvotis' sigh - the heart of the island - are things you will experience only if you wander in the island. A little further, there is **Avlaki** beach and spas.

From Nisyros, you can visit Yiali islet where there is a small village and a very large beach, the main source of pumice stone. There are also Pergousa, Pahia and Strongyli islets which are worth visiting just to complete you trip to the unexpected.

Aerial view to Nikia village and lower on, the Lakki plateau.

TEXT: V. DIKOU &
MARIA ELENI ANTONIOU
TRANSLATION: ARIETA TSAGARAKI
PHOTOS: STAVROS & KOSTAS MARMATAKIS
PRINTING - BINDING:
G. VOULGARIDES - D. CHATZISTILES